Th
B
Alternative
Garden
Wisdom

by Simon Whaley

Zymurgy Publishing, 2007

The moral rights of author Simon Whaley has been asserted.

A CIP catalogue record for this book is available from the British library.

Cover artwork Paul Goldsmith

Cover design Nick Ridley

Printed & bound in Great Britain by
William Clowes Ltd, Beccles, Suffolk
ISBN 978 1903506 264
Published by Zymurgy Publishing,
Newcastle upon Tyne
10 9 8 7 6 5 4 3 2
© Zymurgy Publishing 2007

To Mum

For all those weeds I
pulled up, which were
in the right place after
all.

Simon Whaley has written a number of books some of which have bloomed on best seller lists. He lives in Shropshire where he prunes words and anything else that gets in his way.

www.simonwhaley.co.uk

Contents

"All gardening is landscape-painting"

Alexander Pope

PLOT POTENTIAL

All gardens need a design. Write to every garden makeover show on terrestrial and satellite television but pray that they don't all turn up on the same day. Unless of course you want multi-storey decking.

List everything you want in your newly designed garden.

- Patio for entertaining.
- Barbecue.
- Hot tub.
- Swimming pool.
- Shed (for all the junk that you can't get in the garage).
- Room for the caravan when you're not using it.
- A high concept design feature to make a bold statement and wow the neighbours.
- Oh yeah, and perhaps a plant or two might go down well.

Mother Nature is one of the best garden designers there is. She does it quietly without being asked. Unfortunately, she never seems to win an award at Chelsea though.

When designing your garden, use watercolours and sketch out your plans first.

Have some dreamy music in the background too. Then throw a fancy dress garden-make-over party where friends and family can come dressed as their favourite TV gardening personalities. As well as bringing a bottle, get them to bring a spade or fork too. It's amazing what some people will do if they think they'll be on telly. Make sure that you go dressed as the TV camera man, or better still, disappear for two days and pretend to be the show's surprised 'victim'.

Garden design is a skilled art. A water feature is not an overflowing drainpipe. A compost heap is not the latest creation by next door's cat, and a border is not a small strip of wallpaper that goes around your fencing at waist height.

A garden should be a room for the whole family to enjoy. Ensure that there are sufficient electrical sockets for the children to plug their computer game consoles into.

British soaps like to reflect everyday life, therefore it only makes sense that you should try to reflect the soap storylines. Never lay a patio without having a dead body ready and waiting to put underneath it. Always bury the dead body deep enough — the last thing you want is a patio slab that rocks unevenly from side to side. Someone could trip over it and really hurt themselves!

Low maintenance gardens are very popular with those who don't have time to water, cut the grass, weed the vegetable patch or prune the plants on a regular basis.

The best three steps to a low maintenance garden are:

1.   Buy the top floor flat on a 40 storey block,

2.   Gut your existing garden and completely concrete it over,

3.   Win the lottery and pay someone else to do it.

Garden designs can be categorised in a sliding scale of formality as follows:

* The Country Estate (the Capability Brown approach)
* The Country Estate (the Gertrude Jekyll approach)
* The Walled Garden (looks impressive from the outside approach)
* The Cottage Garden (the haphazard approach)
* The City Garden (the decking approach)
* Au Natural (the easiest approach)

To give a garden impact, always buy enough shrubs and flowers to enable you to plant them in groups of three, five or seven. You'll notice the impact straight away, particularly on your credit card bill.

Gardens should be enjoyed, so always plan ahead. Plant two trees about five metres apart and watch them grow. When ten years have passed, you can string up a hammock between them and then relax and admire all your hard work over the past decade.

Cover up garden eyesores by planting a Russian Vine. Also known as 'mile-a-minute', this fast growing climber is great for hiding sheds, garages, compost areas and complete housing estates.

"What is a weed? A plant whose virtues have not yet been discovered."

Ralph Waldo Emerson

WEED WISDOM

A weed is merely a plant growing in the wrong place. Dig it up and replant it where it should be. (In next door's garden.)

There are two types of chemicals for plants. Good ones and bad ones. Good ones enrich and nourish plants, making them grow miraculously. The other kills, sometimes right down to the root. It's best not to get the two confused, particularly on weeds.

Talking to your plants can help them to grow and thrive, so never talk to weeds. Treat them, as you would your other half.

Weeds need food, water and light, just like any other plant, so applying a layer of mulch around your established plants will help keep them at bay. Mulch is a two-inch layer of organic material (such as bark chippings) which stops light and water reaching any weed seeds in the ground. Think of it as a garden condom. (Just don't ask what a cloche is.)

If you must use a weed killer, use it sparingly…and preferably on weeds. Pay particular attention to that weed growing in the pot on your teenager's bedroom window sill. Weed killer is more effective when it's at this stage – in a pot – as opposed to when it has been dried, cut and rolled up in a small piece of paper. If you do use weed killer when it's in this rolled up stage, stand well back should your teenager try to light it.

Prevent weeds from establishing themselves by covering your soil with a protective membrane. Tiny holes allow light, air and moisture to reach the soil, but they are too small to allow weeds to grow through. Old carpet can be used in much the same way, but if you couldn't live with it inside your house, how do you expect your plants to live with your old flooring cast offs?

Become a crack addict. White powder has its uses. Don't put salt on your freshly grown vegetables when you have them on your dinner plate. Instead, take it outside and pour it down between the gaps in paths and patios. Don't let salt give you high blood pressure, cardiovascular disease or a stroke - let it kill your weeds instead.

"There can be no other occupation like gardening in which, if you were to creep up behind someone at their work, you would find them smiling."

Mirabel Osler

COMPOST CORNER & GRASSCUTTINGS

Compost heaps need heat and moisture to help speed up the composting process. You can help with this by adding your own fresh urine. Early morning is the best time to do this, because the neighbours are less likely to be around.

Shredded paper helps to trap air in your heap, so always mix some in with your grass cuttings. When your credit card company chases you for non-payment of your bill, you can simply explain that your compost heap ate it. Children might like to try this approach with their homework.

Anything that is past its prime and organic will eventually rot down and can therefore be added to a compost heap – except elderly relatives.

Cutting the grass is a man's job. It requires the same spatial awareness skills as driving a car. This is why men always want one of those ride-on lawnmowers when their lawn is only 2 foot square.

Mowing the lawn should be treated like any other Sunday morning ritual, such as washing the car, taking the dog for a walk or having sex with the other half. The quicker you get it done, the sooner you can settle down with the Sunday papers.

Reward your husband's behaviour by giving him the appropriate tools for cutting the grass:

• A ride on mower demonstrates that you have a loving and caring husband because you allow him to tackle this task in the easiest way possible.

• Making your husband cut the lawn with a hover mower means that

he will finish the job in ten minutes.
(You clearly can't trust him on his own
for long periods of time.)

• Hand him a pair of nail
scissors and women up and down the
street will admire your wickedness.
(Although they'll probably be more
intrigued as to what your husband's
misdemeanour was.)

Lawns do not always have to be made from grass. Mary Wesley's popular novel "The Camomile Lawn" has a lawn comprising of this strong smelling herb, which is a main feature of the novel. Many gardeners though are still waiting for a novel entitled "The Clover, Moss, Daisy, Buttercup, Dandelion and Molehill Lawn, with a hint of Grass".

Lawns need aerating from time to time to help drain excess moisture away. You could buy spiked sandals which tie onto your wellington boots, or an aerator that you can push just like a lawnmower.

Forget these – just ask the local under 16's football club to pop around for their next training session. Failing that, get a family member to practice their golf shots in their spiked golf shoes. (Not only will the spikes aerate the ground but also the divots created by a 'slightly off' golf swing will increase the surface area of your lawn, thus improving evaporation.)

There used to be advertisement campaigns suggesting that cutting the grass is a lot less bother with a hover mower. It could be argued that it's even less bother by not having any grass in the first place.

Gardening etiquette dictates that lawns should be mown to produce regimental straight lines. Dedicated male gardeners mow on a Saturday afternoon. Let them tackle it on a Sunday morning and they'll demonstrate to the world how intoxicated they still are after last night's session down the pub with the lads.

Crop rotation helps prevent draining the soil of all its natural goodness and stops diseases from taking a hold. The principle also works well in the greenhouse. Never hide your secret stash of Alan Titchmarsh or Charlie Dimmock pictures in the same place each year in order to avoid detection by nosey members of the family.

All gardens should have a focal point – something to lead the eye through all of the planting to a final resting point of outstanding interest. This can be a tree, an obelisk, a sculpture or even an ornate seat. It should not be your compost heap.

Moles are one of the world's best animals for tunnelling and excavating soil. Don't curse them for ruining your perfectly manicured lawn. Remember some gardeners have to pay good money to have proper drainage installed!

Once your garden has been fully tamed you could open it up to the general public as part of the National Gardens Scheme, which helps to raise money for charity. Ask your neighbours if they mind giving up their tatty front gardens as a possible coach parking facility to help cope with the numbers. There's no need to provide dedicated toilets at such events. Just point visitors in the direction of your compost heap.

"The Glory of the Garden lies in more than meets the eye."

Rudyard Kipling

PRUNING PREDICAMENTS

Leylandii are well known for attaining extreme heights, blocking out light and rain from gardens, plus generally providing enough footage for those devilishly bad neighbour documentaries to last a decade. Always plant Leylandii with extreme caution - at night when no one else is looking.

Deadheading is for faded, wilting flowers - not irritating members of the family.

Pruning helps to tame your plants by making them grow into the shape you want, or to produce more flowers. Learning where to prune can seem confusing. Is it after the second bud on the left after a full moon, or the first bud on the right when there's a Z in the month? Just remember – you are in charge, you are the gardener! Prune it where you like. If the plant doesn't like it, it can just shrivel up and die.

Your local council can instruct you to reduce the height of an overgrown tree, or raise its crown by removing the lower branches, especially if there is a danger to the general public. If you don't, the authority can send a professional lumberjack (or a lumberjill) to carry out the work. In the interests of self-preservation, save all your profanities for when the professionals have their chainsaws switched on (and can't hear you).

Gardening gloves are for wimps. Dedicated rose growers always prune in the nude. Garden twine may be worn though, to help secure drooping body parts. This will prevent any painful snagging. (You can make you own little prick jokes at this point).

Wear gardening belts so that the tool pouch hangs around your side and not your stomach. If you don't, should you bend over, that pair of secateurs could snip something unintentional, or some entirely different undergrowth.

If partners excuse themselves from cutting the hedge because the wooden handles of your garden shears are splintering, wrap some insulating tape around the handles. This will solve the problem. If partners still refuse to cut the hedge, use some more insulating tape to strap their hands to the handles of the shears at the same time.

Box hedging is perfect for creating formal borders in a small and compact area. And you can clip it into almost any shape that you like. Simplicity is the key to style though, so try not to be too complicated with your design. The need to keep titivating with your hedge should be ignored at all cost. A single stalk containing one leaf may well be a modern minimalist design, but it certainly isn't a hedge.

Hedging makes a perfect sound barrier, so plant it wherever you need to stop unwanted noise from entering your garden. It could be from an adjacent main road or the nearby school playing fields. If your topiary skills are up to it, why not shape it into some earmuffs, which you can wear whenever you're outside?

Be an environmentally friendly gardener – never trim or prune your plants. It might look a complete mess to the neighbours, but overgrown gardens absorb more carbon dioxide and give out more oxygen than gravel-covered, minimalist back yards. Let your plants run free and help save the planet from global warming.

Raised beds are a must for anyone with a bad back. They make it easier for getting in and out of, particularly when you've been resting your eyelids after an energetic weeding exercise.

"The book of life begins with a man and a woman in a garden; it ends with revelations."

Oscar Wilde

THE VEGETABLE PLOT THICKENS

Allow plenty of space to grow your vegetables strategically. Think ahead to the presentation table at next year's village show. Remember, male gardeners need two small round vegetables for every long thin one. That's two onions for every marrow, or two Brussels sprouts for every carrot. Men always know how to show off their vegetables in the best light.

One of the easiest ways to mark out a straight line for a border, path, or new vegetable plot, is to tie some garden twine between two canes. Traditional green twine may look camouflaged against the grass or other shrubs, so use something much brighter. The reflective tape used by police forces to mark out a crime scene works well and really gets the neighbours talking!

Gardens can be created in an instant these days by purchasing mature plants from garden centres and supermarkets. If you're trying to create an instant salad garden, remember to buy a whole lettuce, not the pre-washed, prepared bags of leaves. For some reason a row of plastic bags containing mixed salad leaves just doesn't look right.

Tall plants such as runner beans or sweet peas need a frame to climb up. A wigwam shape of gardening canes works well and this is the traditional method. Pioneering gardeners have started using whatever comes to hand, such as clothes props, washing lines or next door's lanky 17 year old who doesn't plan on doing much this summer.

Slugs have a soft underbelly and the slime they excrete helps them to glide over the soft soil. Prevent slugs from reaching your precious vegetables by sticking something sharp around their perimeter. Sand, gravel, even broken egg shells are painful for slugs to cross. The sharp tongue of your next-door neighbour won't work though, no matter how much you'd like it to.

Some gardeners complain that their clay soil is too heavy. The solution is not to pick it up in the first place.

Many traditional gardeners swear that adding compost to your rhubarb improves the flavour. Others swear that adding custard makes it taste better.

"Gardening requires a lot of water — most of it in the form of perspiration."

Lou Erickson

PEST PATROL

Slugs like nothing better than a good slurp of beer or lager. Attract them away from your precious plants by burying a cup in the soil nearby, and then pour in the remnants from your latest six-pack. Lured by the sweet aroma, they simply fall in and drown. Alternatively, consume the entire six-pack yourself and be too sloshed to worry about what the slugs are doing to your plants.

Frighten greenfly from your roses by growing cloves of garlic around them. If that fails, try spearing each fly through the heart with a wooden stake.

Don't throw away your old CD music collection. Scare birds and other pests from your vegetables and fruit by tying CDs to stakes in the ground. As the wind blows them about, the reflections of light dazzle and confuse them. You can scare away unwanted neighbours by simply playing the CDs on your Hi-Fi system at full volume.

You're not the only one doing a little bit of planting in your garden. Squirrels love to bury their nuts in your lawn. Stop them from doing this by concreting your lawned area and then covering it with synthetic turf.

Littering your garden with large stones will enable you to listen to the sounds of murder taking place. Snails might just be slugs with shells, but without something hard to whack them against, Blackbirds and Thrushes can't eat them. Alternatively, boil them with your vegetables and convince yourself that you're eating a French delicacy.

Ringo, George, John and Paul may be friendly, but there are other beetles that gardeners should be worried about. The Cockchafer, Leaf, Pea and Red Lily Beetles would much rather you 'let it be', but if you do, you could be in for 'a hard day's night' and need some 'help!' when you come to inspect the damage that they can do in your garden. The best antidote is a couple of 'rolling stones' to crush them between.

A week after being born, an aphid can produce its own offspring, up to 5 new aphids a day for the next month. The gardener's natural ally is the ladybird, who can eat up to 300 aphids during its larval stage. Welcome your allies with open arms, add a ladybird shelter, rows of hollow bamboo canes or stems, tied together and hidden in a safe dry space in the garden. Give them plenty of reading material. Apparently, ladybirds are also into books about Janet and John.

Some gardeners swear that half a grapefruit skin is a great way of attracting slugs away from your precious plants. That still leaves you with the gruesome task of having to kill them. Instead, throw your grapefruit skins onto your compost heap and grow all of your precious plants under a pine tree. Slugs hate the acidity of fallen pine needles. Think about it. Why attract slugs, when you could deter them in the first place? When was the last time you saw a slug under a pine tree?

Is your garden full of dock leaves? Did your favourite TV Gardener advise you to use a grubber? Have you just bent the prongs trying to get it out? Who says TV Gardeners know everything? Instead, turn your garden into a smallholding. Pigs will unearth the roots and sheep like the leaves for the vitamins they contain. Next time you see a dock leaf, don't call it a weed. Think of it as a selenium and zinc crop for sheep.

"All really grim gardeners possess a keen sense of humus."

WC Sellar and RJ Yeatman

GREENHOUSE GROUNDINGS

Greenhouses with lichen-covered panes are the best. It has nothing to do with improved plant propagation – it just saves embarrassing the neighbours. Well how else are you supposed to water your tomatoes when there's a hosepipe ban on?

Keep up with the camaraderie between fellow gardeners. Always give away extra plants and cuttings that you no longer have room for in the greenhouse. This helps to make more room for new plants. Quickly plant up any that you receive from fellow gardeners, otherwise you might inadvertently give the same plant back a few weeks later.

Railway sleepers are excellent as retaining walls for raised beds, steps and even decking. Where would gardeners be without them? (Where would our railways be with them?) Next time you're in the greenhouse, raise a toast to Dr Beeching - the patron saint of recycled garden structures.

Greenhouses are for growing things, like ideas, dreams and fantasies. Nurture them regularly, particularly if they involve your favourite TV gardener watering your plants whilst naked.

Garden bulbs come in two varieties, so knowing which is which will enhance your garden immensely. Daffodils, snowdrops and crocus bulbs need planting the right way up and at the right depth to ensure that they stay warm over winter. The other type of bulb only comes to life when connected to a power supply.

Save money by collecting your own seeds, but only do this from healthy looking plants. This will help prevent the spread of disease. To check whether a plant is healthy, ask it to open its mouth and say "Aah".

Finding new plants is always a joy to gardeners but some unscrupulous plant smiths help themselves to 'cuttings' when no one is looking and hide them in a bag. This is wrong, so don't do it, because the cutting may die before you get it home. Instead, line a plastic box with some wet tissues before you go out, and this will help the cutting to obtain moisture, until you can propagate it properly back at home.

Espostoa Lanata is every schoolchild's favourite cactus. (Suffice to say it has a very rude male anatomical shape.)

Grapevines grow well in a greenhouse or a conservatory, but don't let the grapes get sunburnt. Pick them early enough and give them to someone in hospital who will really appreciate them – like the person who fell off the ladder in the first place trying to pick them.

If your neighbour asks you for advice on what to do with his wilting cucumber, be gentle with him. It may not amount to much, but it might be all he has left. Suggest carefully that it should be kept hidden at all times, rather than left out in the open for all to see.

"The kiss of the sun for
pardon,
The song of the birds for
mirth,
One is nearer God's
heart in a garden,
Than anywhere else on
earth."

Dorothy Frances Gurney

WILDLIFE WONDERS

Birdfeeders help attract birds into your garden. Hang them from branches but ensure they are high enough so that cats can't reach them. Remember where they are, otherwise the next time you mow the lawn you might knock yourself out on one. And then you'll miss the cartoon birds circling around your head.

Wooden seats around tree trunks are the perfect way to survey your handy work at the end of the day. They also make you a perfect sitting duck for the full bowels of the birds sitting in the branches above.

If you're going to tame the birds, then you may end up taming the squirrels too. Remember, these are intelligent creatures who really enjoy running along washing lines, jumping through hoops, standing on pressure pads, which raise barriers so they can press a button to release a nut for them to hide somewhere. If that's too complicated for you to set up, just give them your credit card so that the squirrels can order their own nuts online.

Attracting birds into your garden will keep insect pests under control in an organic way. Stick up some bird boxes to encourage them to stay. Naming your boxes may attract specific birds. Bra Cottage (Tits), Retirement Home for Female World War II Veterans (Wrens) and Hungry House (Swallows).

Ponds are a great feature for gardens, attracting wildlife and providing a habitat for a whole new range of plants. Large ponds can also become natural swimming pools for the warmer months when you need to cool down after a hard day's work in the garden. Fish, toads and frogs do not appreciate a gardener's attempt at turning natural swimming pools into natural Jacuzzis. Always swim before eating a meal, especially if it's a high fibre one.

Keep ponds algae free by stuffing an old pair of tights with some barley straw and then weighting it down in the water. Some scientists believe that the chemical properties of barley prevent algae from growing. Lay people know that in reality, anything in old tights is enough to frighten away all living organisms.

During winter, when ponds freeze over, the pressure of the ice as the water expands can damage the pond liner or container. Float something on the surface to help absorb some of this pressure, such as a football, a log, or one of the in-laws.

Never let children help remove blanket weed from a pond, because this can be a dangerous place for them. Instead let them play peacefully in the garden. When you stretch too far and fall in, enjoy the panic that ensues as they watch you re-emerge bogey-monster-like from the depths of the pond, covered in blanket and duck weed.

Get a bee nesting box for your garden, and help bees hibernate over winter. In the spring, they help to pollinate your trees, flowers and herbs, which create the garden you enjoy so much. Unfortunately, they also help to pollinate dandelions, daises and other weeds. Well how is a bee supposed to know whether a plant is in the right place or not?

Birds need to keep clean too, so if you don't have a pond, install a birdbath. The incessant flapping of wings as they wash will shower the surrounding plants and help to water them. (There's no need to install showers, Jacuzzis or bidets, birds are just interested in the bath.)

Consider using an old tin bath in your garden as a water feature. Fill it with water, install a few fish, add some pond plants such as water lilies, or water hyacinths and watch the frogs, toads and newts move in. It's best to wait until Granddad has finished using it, dried himself and got dressed, before making a start.

"Perennials are the ones that grow like weeds, biennials are the ones that die this year instead of next and hardy annuals are the ones that never come up at all."

Katharine Whitehorn

A GARDENER'S GLOSSARY

Perennial. A non-woody plant, which will live for two or more years. In other words, it'll require pruning, thinning, dividing or dead heading just to get the most benefit. (A bit like kids really.)

Annual. A plant, which has its whole life cycle in one growing season, from seed germination, to flowering and dying. It's perfect for the fashion conscious gardener who wants to grow this year's "in" flowers, before having to start all over again next year. Annuals are the gardener's treadmill.

Hardy Annual. An annual plant capable of surviving a frost. Great! You can stick it in the ground before May is out.

Half Hardy Annual. An annual plant, which may not be able to withstand a frost. Bugger it – shove it in the ground before May is out and let it take its chances.

Biennial. A plant, which requires two growing seasons — the first to produce the leaf growth, the second to produce the flower. So plant it and forget it, but try not to pull it up next year as a weed.

Climbers and Trailers. Perfect plants for hiding hideous walls and buildings in a riot of colour as they spread across a structure. It's usually a vigorous weed from next door's garden that devours entire sheds, which are never seen again.

Rockery. An area of high stone and low soil content where some alpine plants have adapted to survive in these minimal conditions. In reality, it's usually the corner of your garden used by the building contractors of your housing estate as the dumping ground for broken bricks and masonry, which you can't be bothered to clear.

Bulbs. A giant seed, producing a riot of colour for one season of the year before dying back and remaining unseen until next year. As a result, you can never remember where they are until you accidentally dig one up when trying to plant something else in that spot.

Ha Ha. Popular in large country estates, it's a hidden embankment used as a retaining wall without spoiling any of the views from the garden. It's called a "Ha Ha" because that's what everyone says when you inadvertently fall over it because you're too busy looking at the view.

"But though an old man, I am but a young gardener."

Thomas Jefferson

GARDEN CUTTINGS

Global warming means that gardens of the future will be different because traditional species will not be able to survive in the higher temperatures. This means that in the UK, plants from the Mediterranean and Africa may be able to survive. Prepare for this now by stripping your garden of everything and replacing it all with sand. Wait for the temperatures to rise and the heat to become so unbearable that your mind starts playing tricks on you. Well, whoever heard of a horrible mirage?

Watering plants sparingly encourages their taproots to develop and bury themselves deeper into the ground in search of moisture. This produces a much stronger plant capable of enduring drier conditions. Why water your plants when their tap roots could bury through the planet and someone on the other side of the world can do your watering for you?

Newly created rockeries or patios can look obviously new, so to speed up the ageing process, spread natural yoghurt on the bare rock surfaces. This encourages smaller organisms such as lichens to grow and prematurely age the rocks. Remember to keep the household pets indoors otherwise, they may just lick all the yoghurt off, defeating the exercise.

Plants can be used to spell out words and phrases. Combine your love of plants with your love of words and show your neighbourhood the full extent of your vocabulary. As your gardening knowledge expands try moving onto five letter words.

Exhibiting your prize blooms

in the village show requires intense preparation beforehand. Paper bags are what you need. Cover each of your prize flowers with a paper bag just before they bloom, and tie it to the stem with a wire twist tie. This will stop insects and birds from damaging the petals. Keep it on until show day and remove the paper bag when you're ready to exhibit. Have an extra large paper bag to put over your own head in case your blooms don't win you first prize.

The sound of running water

can add a beautiful feature and charm to your garden, unless of course, you're dying for a pee. Thereafter the sound of more running water will probably bring a temporary pollution problem, if not relief, unless of course, you happen to be near the compost heap.

Plants can be damaged by sudden, huge gusts of wind, so consider installing windbreaks to protect them. Alternatively don't bend over quite so quickly, because this reduces the risk of your body producing such breezes.

If an Englishman's home is his castle, then that makes the garden a country estate. Act like Lady of the Manor and get a man in to do the gardening. Whilst interviewing, assess your potential under gardener's physical attributes (for difficult landscaping jobs) and his knowledge of reference material ... The Gardener's Encyclopaedia of Plants & Flowers ... Flora Britannica ... Lady Chatterley's Lover ...

Women water gardens better than men do. They tend to sprinkle daintily from large rose tipped watering cans, whilst men shoot from the hip with trigger guns on the end of hoses. Mother Nature sprinkles from the heavens above, and is therefore the best example to follow. Never let a man do the watering. If his aim in the bathroom (whether he lifts the seat or not) is anything to go by, the chances are, his aim with a hose in the garden is just as poor.

Taming a garden takes more than one season. Many Gardeners are aware of this and break the year down into gardening themed jobs. Therefore, instead of referring to the seasons as Spring, Summer, Autumn and Winter, they may refer to them as Pruning, Mowing, Leaf Sweeping and Digging.

What does your garden say about you? Some psychologists believe that your garden is an extension of your personality. A neat and tidy garden is the product of a neat and tidy mind. The chaotic beauty of a cottage garden suggests a dreamy but erratic thought process. A garden full of children suggests that you enjoy growing seeds in a completely different kind of bed.

Understanding the food cycle

in your garden can help you to eradicate pests. Worms eat decomposing organic material, ladybirds are great aphid killers, hedgehogs like slugs and worms, whilst many birds eat worms and insects, before tackling your own vegetable garden produce. Pigeons in particular will take a shine to your cabbages and broccoli. Why don't you take a shine to those pigeons before they eat your cabbage? Your cabbage will taste even sweeter when eaten with Pigeon Pie.

"Gardening is a matter of your enthusiasm holding up until your back gets used to it."

Anonymous

THE POTTING SHED

A dibber is a delightful tool, usually made of wood, which allows you to dib it into the ground to make a small hole. (What's wrong with your finger?) This makes it easier to transfer young seedlings direct into the ground for planting on. Gardeners doing this during summer in clay soil may find a pneumatic drill achieves the same result.

Always obtain time-saving tools. It's possible to buy forks with pre-bent prongs to break up the soil between plants. This is so much easier than buying a fork and trying to bend the prongs yourself.

Robins prefer perching on the old fashion D shaped tool handles as opposed to the modern T shaped ones. Plant your D shaped handled fork into your vegetable path and watch the robin fly to it. Move it about the patch from time to time, to make the neighbours think you're actually working your land.

Blower Vacs are great for collecting dead leaves off the ground in the autumn. They help to keep your garden looking pristine. But they're even better at sucking spiders out of the bath.

If you can't afford a Blower Vac to collect leaves, put your lawn aerator shoes on and use the spikes to spear the leaves as you aerate your lawn.

Keep garden twine in your pocket at all times. You'll never know when you'll need to tie up any gangly, uncontrollable growths like climbing roses, runner beans or loose children.

Fashions come and fashions go and the perfect place to keep up to date is at your local garden centre. Try on the latest gardening clogs or wellies and test out waterproof jackets. Remember, your garden path is your catwalk. Last year's cast offs can be used by the scarecrow in your vegetable plot. Well let's face it — last year's fashions are enough to scare anything away.

Always carry one of those Swiss army style penknives with you. They have a selection of blades to take cuttings, a corkscrew so you can enjoy the odd illegal tipple from your private greenhouse supply, a saw to lop branches off trees, tweezers for getting rose thorns out of fingers and one of those long pointy thingamajigs for getting stones out of horse's hooves. If you don't see any horses, don't panic. This tool is perfect for spearing slugs who venture too close to your plants.

The size of your butt is something to be proud of.
(Your water butt, that is.)

Slash and Burn. This is what dogs do to ruin your lawn.

Potting sheds are for potting up plants, not growing pot in.

Every gardener should have an endless supply of plastic fizzy drinks bottles. They can be used for:

a) Watering plants in confined spaces (use the whole bottle)

b) Mini cloches for individual cuttings (use the bottom half of the bottle)

c) Pest control around young seedlings (use the middle as a collar)

d) Somewhere to store your secret homebrew in (use the whole bottle)

e) A useful receptacle if caught short whilst out in the garden. (don't get this mixed up with the bottles in 'd')

"When weeding, the best way to make sure you are removing a weed and not a valuable plant is to pull on it. If it comes out of the ground easily, it is a valuable plant."

Anonymous